DEAR FASHION

diary

BY EMMI OJALA
&
LAURA DE JONG

BISPUBLISHERS

BIS Publishers

Building Het Sieraad

Postjesweg 1

1057 DT Amsterdam

The Netherlands

T +31 (0)20 515 02 30

F +31 (0)20 515 02 39

bis@bispublishers.nl

www.bispublishers.nl

ISBN 978 90 6369 310 7

THIS BOOK BELONGS TO

NAME: _____

AGE: _____

WORDS / *things* that describe me:

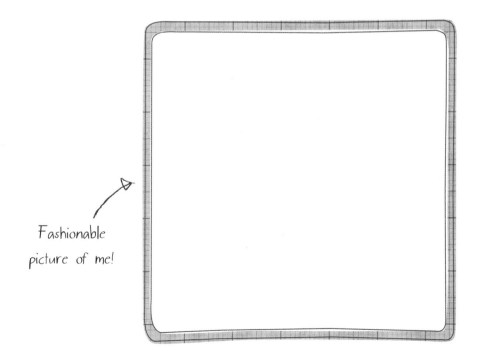

Fashionable
picture of me!

dear

your name here

This is your very own fashion diary, offline blog and personal collection of inspiration that will lead you off the beaten tracks of fashion! Keep it private, share it with friends, start filling it from the beginning or from the end. The only real fashion rule is that there is none, and the same goes for this book! All you need to do is pick up a pen and a stick of glue to fill this diary with your doodles, notes and collages.

To navigate through the list of contents, turn to the last pages of this book to find the right pages for sharing your wildest fashion dreams and learning how to take care of your clothes!

Show us what you did with your diary and share your creativity online at Facebook.com/DearFashionDiary or Twitter.com/DearFashionBook!

LET`S KICK OFF with a mini-interview. Answer these three questions with DOODLES and *letters*!

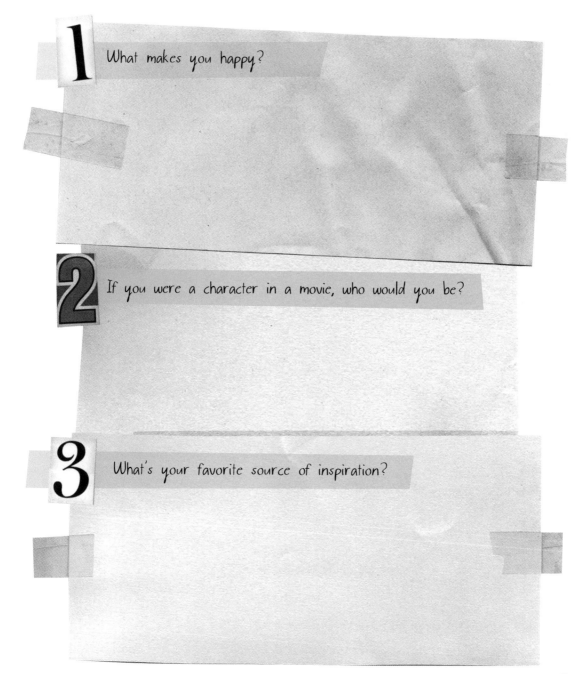

1 What makes you happy?

2 If you were a character in a movie, who would you be?

3 What's your favorite source of inspiration?

STYLE TIMELINE

Pen your earliest, funniest and the
best fashion memories on this timeline!

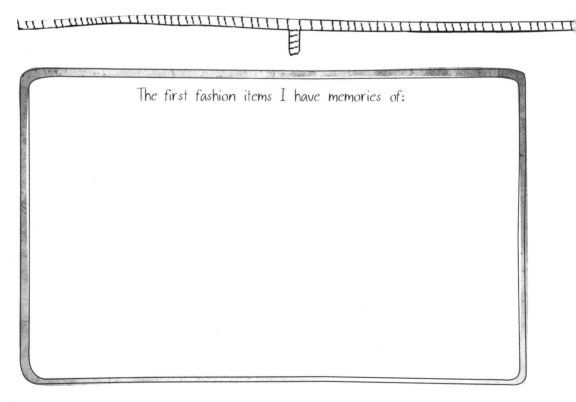

The first fashion items I have memories of:

When I was young, my favorite clothes were

I loved them because

I ☐ liked ☐ disliked dressing up, and ☐ always ☐ never wanted to wear

My first style icon

When I started school,
these things were trendy:

People, places and events that have influenced my style:

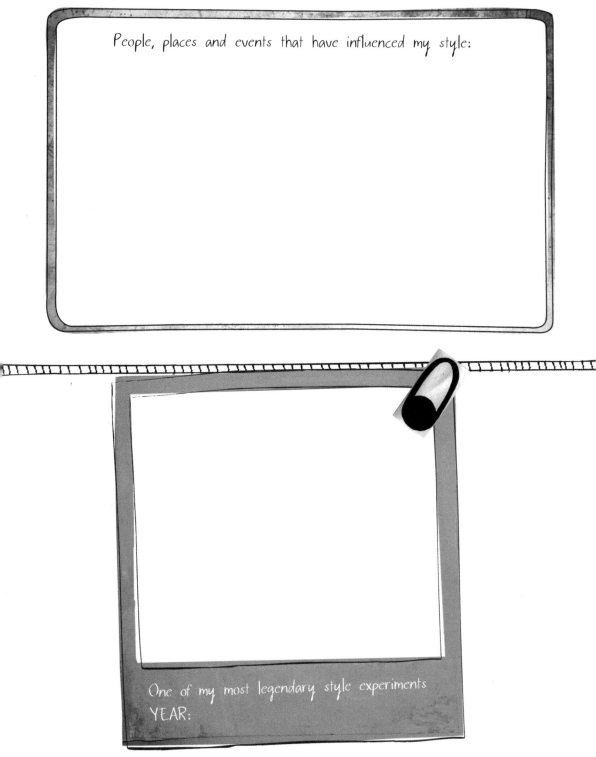

One of my most legendary style experiments
YEAR:

In the past years, my style has become more

I have been inspired by

The words that best describe my current style are

If my style was a book, it would be titled

In ten years, I see my future self wearing outfits like this:

OUTFIT MEMORABILIA

Share the story behind a special outfit that holds treasured memories from an important moment in your life.

One of my dearest, most memorable outfits is this

I got it from

and wore it when

It made me feel

and still reminds me of

I will never forget that day, because

Attach an image of
your special outfit here!

CLOTHING calculus

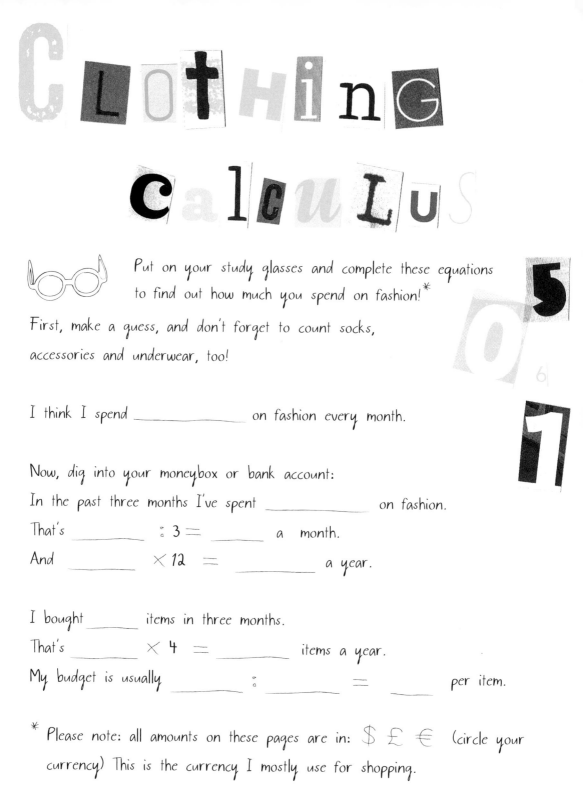

Put on your study glasses and complete these equations to find out how much you spend on fashion!*

First, make a guess, and don't forget to count socks, accessories and underwear, too!

I think I spend _____ on fashion every month.

Now, dig into your moneybox or bank account:

In the past three months I've spent _____ on fashion.

That's _____ : 3 = _____ a month.

And _____ × 12 = _____ a year.

I bought _____ items in three months.

That's _____ × 4 = _____ items a year.

My budget is usually _____ : _____ = _____ per item.

* Please note: all amounts on these pages are in: $ £ € (circle your currency) This is the currency I mostly use for shopping.

Did you know: most women wear only
20% of their wardrobe 80% of the time.

If I bought only this 20% of my clothes
I would spend _____ × 0,2 = _____ per year.   9

And I would buy only _____ × 0,2 = _____ items.

If I spent the same amount of money on buying only 20% of the number
of items that I usually buy now, my budget would be

_____ : _____ = _____ per item.

shopaholic
average
you

Women spend around

$ 1000 / £ 625 / € 770

on fashion per year.

How much do you spend
per year compared to
women on average?

Complete this diagram accordingly.

My target budget for the coming year is _____
so I will try to spend max _____ : 12 = _____ on fashion per month.

SHOPPING
SABBATICAL

DO YOU want to take your fashion creativity even further? You could challenge yourself to go on a shopping *sabbatical* to find alternative ways of updating your wardrobe. Go on, take the dare: it might be more fun than you think!

Tip:
Use this contract to set the rules
for your own challenge:
Are you allowed to buy second-hand?
Can you swap clothes with others?
Does buying new jewellery count as well?

MY SHOPPING SABBATICAL CONTRACT

I _____ hereby declare that

I will not shop for _____ days/weeks/months/years.

My shopping sabbatical will start on _____

and will end on _____ .

My personal rules

☐ _____

☐ _____

☐ _____

☐ _____

Signature _____

Date _____

WARDROBE INVENTORY

REVEAL the contents of your closet
and count ALL the items in it!

...... *tops*   ...... _____
...... PAIRS OF SHOES   ...... _____
...... *jackets*   ...... _____
...... _____   ...... _____
...... _____   ...... _____
...... _____   ...... _____
...... _____   ...... _____
...... _____   ...... _____
...... _____   ...... _____
...... _____   ...... _____
...... _____   ...... _____
...... _____   ...... _____
...... _____   ...... _____
...... _____

                                 ...... TOTAL

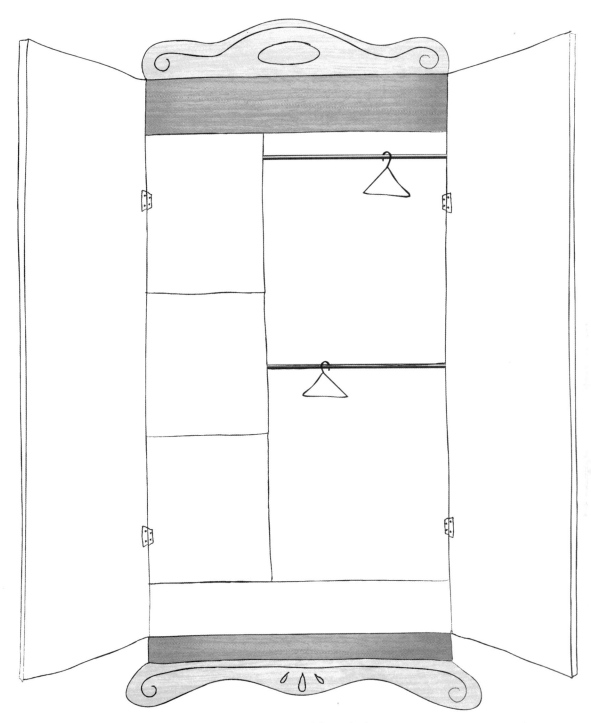

This wardrobe is yours to fill: hang, fold and draw your garments in it!

HELLO WORLD

GRAB a pile of your clothes and take a look at the 'made in' label inside. Where do the makers of your clothing live?

Place them as dots on this map.

FASHION

Put together an exhibition with your oldest garments and write a bio for them!

MUSEUM

Item:

Year of purchase:

Description:

Item:

Year of purchase:

Description:

Item:

Year of purchase:

Description:

Item:

Year of purchase:

Description:

Item:

Year of purchase:

Description:

REPORT

by museum curator

My oldest garments are

I wear them often/rarely/from time to time and will never say

goodbye to them, unless

My all-time favorite among my golden oldies is

I would love to find something with the same

I hope that the following garments from my current wardrobe

will age well and become part of my fashion museum in ten years'

time:

DATE

SIGNATURE

WHAT MAKES A GARMENT OUTDATED?

Write down your answer:

"Old does not mean outdated"

– Filippa K

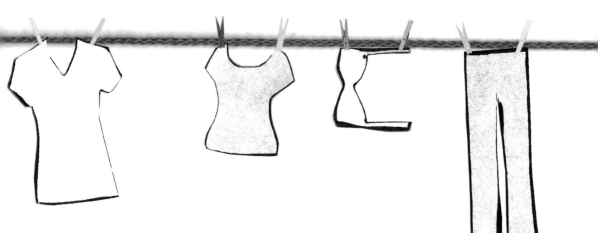

MY

COLORS

DOES YOUR wardrobe look like the closet of a colorful chameleon or that of a black panther? Reveal the colors inside your wardrobe.

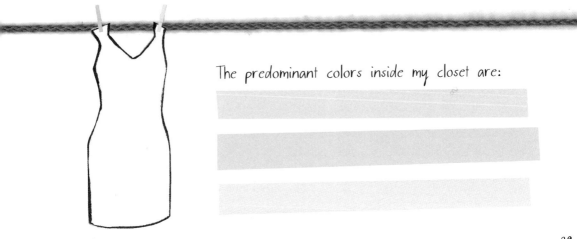

The predominant colors inside my closet are:

MY IDEAL COLORS

Is your *wardrobe* filled with bright candy colors or plain vanilla hues that don't fit your style? Use this color fan to create a color palette that better matches your style!

Tip: Use this as your
color chart when shopping!

My ideal colors

DIAMONDS ARE A GIRL'S BEST FRIEND

Are you a girl with pearl earrings and diamond rings or do you prefer plastic fantastic? Reveal the contents of your jewellery box and doodle your trinkets on this page!

closet confessions...

ARE YOU a hoarder of 🎩 s or a 👠
fanatic? Come out with your biggest fashion
fetishes! Go ahead, draw pictures of them **ALL** !

PSST

...feel free to glue these pages together
if your confession is of an aukward
kind...

love song

We all have our favorite garments: write your dearest a love song!

This song is dedicated to my

because

lyrics: _____

don't forget the chorus!

GALLERY OF CATASTROPHES

Everyone makes mistakes, also with fashion. What are the clothes that you are most ashamed of? Fill this gallery with your mispurchases, the clothes that you never wear and shouldn't have bought to begin with.

Item:

Why you have it in your closet:

Why you never wear it:

Item:

Why you have it in your closet:

Why you never wear it:

Item:

Why you have it in your closet:

Why you never wear it:

Item:

Why you have it in your closet:

Why you never wear it:

Item:

Why you have it in your closet:

Why you never wear it:

WHAT WAS I THINKING

Well, these mispurchases are quite funny...

I wonder what I was thinking when I bought them, that they would really

_____ ?

Well, it seems I better avoid _____ in the future. I guess

that makes sense, I'd rather wear _____ anyway.

From now on, I should be more selective about _____

and _____ when shopping. Although not all

my mispurchases are utterly bad: at least _____

and _____ will get a second chance,

as I will _____

TEST: HOW HAPPY ARE YOUR CLOTHES?

What's the level of happiness inside your wardrobe?
Complete this quiz to find out!

YES   NO

1 Are your knits neatly folded in your closet? ☐ ☐
2 Do your jeans visit the washing machine
  less than once a month? ☐ ☐
3 Do you have more than one pair of everyday shoes? ☐ ☐
4 Do you use a shoehorn? ☐ ☐
5 Do you own leather protectant spray? ☐ ☐
6 Have your leather items become acquainted with it? ☐ ☐
7 Do you fix holes immediately when they appear? ☐ ☐
8 Have you aired out some of your clothes after wearing
  them in the past two weeks? ☐ ☐

Count the YES-boxes you ticked to find out the results!

0-1 Oh dear, your clothes are looking sad!
    Cheer them up by treating them well!
2-4 Room for improvement!
5-6 If your clothes could smile, they would look
    pretty satisfied. Try to make their smile even wider!
7-8 There is happy bunch living inside your closet!

Make your clothes the happiest ones in your household!

List the things you could do to take better care of them:

TAKE CARE

BY TREATING your clothes kindly, you can prolong their lifespan by years! Here is how to provide tender care for your precious ones:

Darling knits:

Keep your dear knits folded on a shelf to keep them from stretching out of shape. Tackle lint balls and fuzz with duct tape by pressing the sticky side of the tape on your item and peeling back. If the tape doesn't help, go to your closest department store and ask for a lint remover. You can also try to raze the lint off with a razor blade, but be careful not to harm your clothing (or yourself)!

Sweet jeans:

If your jeans aren't actually dirty, introduce them to the great outdoors and air them out instead of washing. When you have to wash your jeans for real, turn them inside out and use cool water to preserve their color.

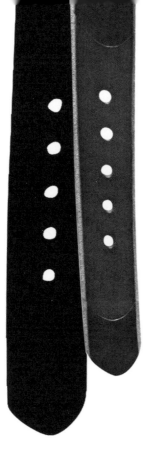

Leather lovelies:

Take care of your leather items by spraying them with water and stain protectant and by giving them a full treatment every four months: remove stains with a moist cloth and prevent drying out and cracking by rubbing the items with leather conditioner. If your items start losing their color, apply colored leather balm on the worn-out areas. Pair your leather jacket up with your best hanger to keep it from wrinkling.

Suede shoes:

Spray your shoes with water and stain protectant and avoid wearing them when it is raining cats and dogs. Wrap them in tissue paper and keep inside your closet away from humidity. Neaten your shoes up with a brush to get rid of dust, mud stains and scuff marks.

Tip:
Remember to give your shoes a break and avoid wearing the same pair two days in a row!

WASH WITH FONDNESS

All you need is a full laundry basket, a laundry machine and detergent. Let's get your laundry done!

1. Sort out your dirty clothes, making separate piles for whites, bright colors and darks. Close the zippers and empty the pockets as you go. Make sure to take out the most delicate garments such as lingerie and the ones marked with 'dry-clean only'.

2. Start with one of the piles and choose the right washing powder for it; you may have different detergents for the whites and the colors. Check the detergent package for instructions and measure the right amount for your washing machine. Keep in mind that detergents tend to be very concentrated these days, so use them sparingly; adding more soap than necessary doesn't make your laundry any cleaner.

3. Forget the fabric softener; there is no real need for it and it is also harmful to the environment.

4. Check the care label of your garments for the highest water temperature they can handle. Note that this is the maximum temperature; you are allowed to wash at a lower temperature, too, which is better for your garment, energy bill and the environment.

5. Put the clothes inside your laundry machine and choose the right program (check the washing symbols on the right) and press start.

30	machine wash
30	machine wash cold/ cool delicate cycle
30	machine wash cold/ cool wool cycle
	hand wash in lukewarm water
	do not wash
	do not bleach
P F	dry clean only
	no dry clean

	do not tumble-dry
	tumble-dry, low heat
	tumble-dry, medium heat
	do not iron
	iron at low heat
	iron at medium heat
	iron at high heat

6. After the wash has finished, hang or lay your garments on a drying rack. A natural air-dry is the best for your clothes and will save energy as well, so there is no need for tumble-drying!

7. Once your clothes have dried, fold your clean laundry and put them in your closet. Yes, you got that right, we didn't mention ironing. If you really really really want to iron your clothes, don't let us stop you, but keep in mind it's bad for your clothes and energy bill.

DIY WASH

LEARN to wash like back in the days when laundry machines didn't exist and follow this hand wash tutorial to clean the most delicate of your fashion items!

WHAT YOU NEED

- a bucket big enough for your laundry
- (liquid) laundry soap
- water
- rubber gloves

NOTE: This tutorial is suitable for all clothes except the ones that require dry-cleaning!

1. Prepare for the manual DIY wash by collecting your lace knickers, woolen socks and other items made of delicate materials.

2. Fill your bucket with water. Cool water is usually the best option for most fabrics (and your energy bill), so use hot water only if you need to kill the bacteria in your socks.

3. Pour the laundry soap in. If you are using powder, dissolve it in the water by mixing. Put your clothes in the bucket and add water till they are covered.

4. Take a break and polish your nails or dance around the house to let the clothes soak for 20 minutes.

5. Pull on your rubber gloves and knead your clothes gently as if you were kneading bread. Take the clothes out and let the water drain off. Empty the bucket and put the clothing back in it. Add clean water until they are covered and knead again to get rid of the soap. You might have to repeat this twice to remove all the detergent.

6. Drain the clothes and hang them to dry. Remember to be kind to your knits and dry them on a flat surface; this way they won't stretch out of shape.

TIPS

- To avoid accidental felting, wash your woolen items gently in cold water without rubbing.

- New, never-washed items are likely to leak color, so play safe and wash them separately! Older clothes that you trust not to leak can be washed together no matter the color.

HOW TO FIX BUTTONS

Grab a needle and a piece of thread, follow
this tutorial and find the fun in sewing!

1. If your button is missing, search the inside of your garment for a spare. If you can't find one, buy a new button with a similar shape and color as the original. You can also choose a special design to make a statement with your button as long as you make sure it will fit through the buttonhole.

2. Find yourself some thread in the same color as the button or choose a contrasting tone for a quirky detail. Believe it or not, you will need as much as 30 centimeters of thread to sew on a button; that's the length of a traditional school ruler.

3. Tie a knot at the end of the thread and slip the other end through the eye of your needle. Make two stitches in the shape of a X about 3 millimeters wide.

4. Hold the button close to the fabric. Stitch upward through the fabric and through one buttonhole, and then through the hole diagonally across from the first one.

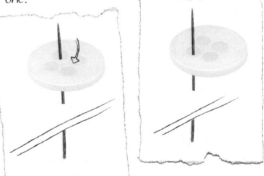

5. Bring the needle up and back through the other holes and repeat four times. Wrap the remaining thread around the back of the button, creating a small stem. Push the needle through the stem a few times and then tie the thread.

Practice here!

Tip: When a button falls off, leave the remaining pieces of thread on your garment; this way it will be easy for you to find the right place for the button when you sew it back on!

RECIPES FOR STAIN REMOVAL

If you stain your clothes, there's no need to cry; applying a few easy tricks can save many hopeless stain situations. Here is how to become the savior of your clothes!

WHAT YOU NEED

- Salt for absorbing liquids
- Dishwashing soap
- Piece of cloth for blotting
- Milk to give ink stains a milky bath

Red wine & blood stains:

Sprinkle salt on the stained area in order to soak up the liquid. Then let cold water do the trick. Remove blood stains by blotting the area with cold water until the stain fades away and get rid of wine smudges by soaking the fabric in cold water for an hour. Finish by washing as usual.

Lipstick:

Apply dish wash detergent.

Greasy spots:

Tackle fresh oil stains and grease smudges by covering them with salt. After the salt has done its duty and absorbed the grease, remove it gently and apply another layer to salt the stain until it fades away. After that, launder as usual.

Ink:

Rub the fresh stain with salt, take the milk from your fridge and prepare a milk bath for your garment. Soak it overnight and wash as usual in the morning.

Bubblegum:

Put your clothing in the freezer and wait for an hour. Take it out and simply scratch the frozen chewing gum away!

Stubborn stains on white fabric:

In extreme cases of stubborn stains, try ox gall soap, a natural stain remover. If that doesn't help, you can try bleaching the stain with chlorine, but remember to be careful - chemicals are not to be messed around with!

For trickier stains, questions and mental support, call your personal helpline (mothers are recommended).

Write the number down here!

EMERGENCY NUMBER:

SPRING CLEANING

FREE YOUR CLOSET from dust bunnies and unworn rags and do a thorough spring cleaning!

WHAT YOU NEED

- your favorite playlist
- duster
- crew members with good fashion sense
- cookies for tea breaks

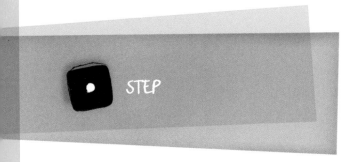

STEP

- Turn on the music and empty your wardrobe. Grab a duster and wipe the shelves, then organize your clothes into three piles:

1. CLOTHES YOU *love*

2. CLOTHES WITH THE WRONG *shape / size*

3. CLOTHES YOU BARELY EVER WEAR

- Put the first pile back into your
  wardrobe and leave the second one aside.
- Give a private fashion show to your
  crew members by wearing the clothes from the third pile.
  Let them judge which of the garments should still get
  a chance to stay in your closet.
- Fold the chosen pieces and put them back into your wardrobe.
  Be sure to place them in a visible spot so that you won't forget to
  wear them!
- Reward your jury with cookies and let them dig through the remaining
  clothes in the second and the third pile to find something for themselves.

STEP

- Invite friends, neighbors and strangers to a *fashion party*:
  Be the matchmaker between them and the clothes you don't need.

STORE the remaining clothes away
in a box. Take them to the closest
recycling center, donate to charity or
keep for DIY projects!

excuse labels

YOU LOVED ME...
10 years ago

I was just really cheap

BE TRUTHFUL to yourself (and your closet!) and use these excuse labels to mark the items that don't belong in your wardrobe anymore!

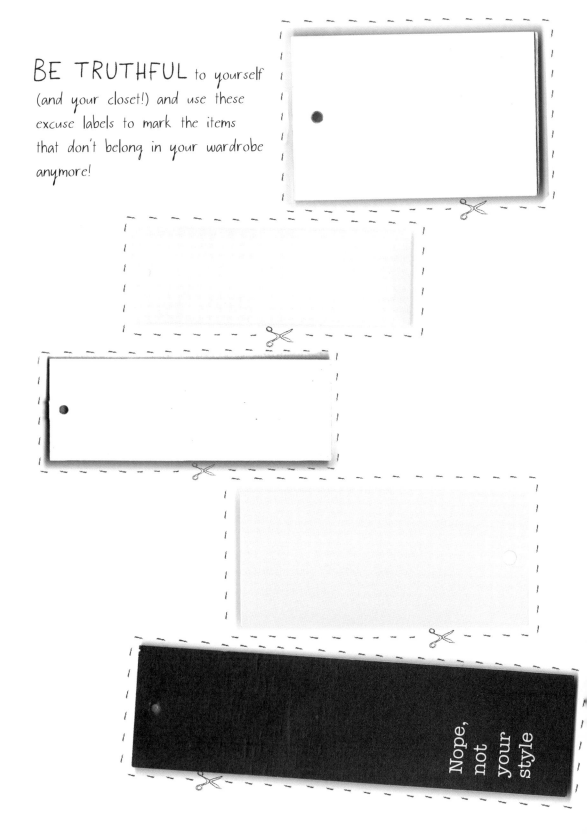

Nope, not your style

be trendy, not spendy

PICK your favorite fashion trends and make a list of their characteristics. Then dive into your wardrobe and steal the look by using your old items!

Glue some images of the trend here!

Glue an image of
your own interpretation of the trend here!

Description of the trend:

Colors:

Materials:

Silhouette:

Must-have ingredients:

Description of the trend:

Colors:

Materials:

Silhouette:

Must-have ingredients:

Glue some images of the trend here!

Glue an image of
your own interpretation of the trend here!

WHAT MAKES SOMEONE WELL-DRESSED?

Write down your answer!

" It's not money that makes you well dressed, it's understanding"

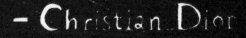

– Christian Dior

CLOSET CRUSH

WHOSE closet would you like to have
in the wardrobe swap of your dreams?

If I could change wardrobes with anyone, I would like to have the

closet of _____

_____

because _____

_____

_____

_____

What makes me excited about his/her closet is _____

_____

_____

_____

Cut, paste and draw pictures
of the outfits and items you
would get in the swap!

SWAP PARTY

Throw a fashionable potluck party and celebrate fashion by swapping clothes! Here is how to become the hostess with the mostess:

1 Invitations

Set a date and time for the party. Copy and cut out the invitations on the next page. Give these to friends, family and neighbors.

> Tip: Making sure that everyone will find something to bring home from your swapping party will be easier if the party is held as a private VIP celebration rather than a public event. 10-15 guests would be ideal.

2 Preparations

Find safety pins and cut out pieces of paper to make labels for the clothes brought to the party. Make sure you have some clothing racks, hangers and space for displaying the garments. Get one or two big mirrors and pick a room to be used as a fitting room. Collect cups and plates to cater for everyone and stock up on drinks and snacks. Don't forget to choose the right party tunes for your stereo either!

3 Kick-off

When your guests have arrived, lay out all the clothes. Attach the labels to the garments and ask their owners to write a wish for the new owner, for example 'May this dress bring elegance to your style'. Once the museum of clothes and little wishes is set up, invite everyone to see and try on each other's clothes.

4 Auction

When your guests have tried on the clothes they like, gather everyone together and start a fashion auction. Go through the clothes one by one, asking who would be interested in having them. Try to make sure that everybody gets at least one thing they like: compromising and being fair is the key!

5 Catwalk celebration

When the auction is over, celebrate together by wearing your new clothes and strutting around the room like supermodels! You can also organize a little panel discussion to let everyone explain where and how they are planning to wear the items.

6 Ending

Negotiate what to do with the remaining clothes. If their owners don't want to take them back home, donate them to a local charity or bring them to a second-hand store.

SWAP PARTY INVITE

Dear _____

You and the clothes that you don't need anymore are invited to _____'s
swap party, where we will have fun by exchanging fashion items and finding
new owners for our old garments!

Please bring

Date _____   ☐ Yourself, some clothes and a happy mood
Time _____   ☐ Something to drink
Place _____ ☐ Something to snack

SWAP PARTY INVITE

Dear _____

You and the clothes that you don't need anymore are invited to _____'s
swap party, where we will have fun by exchanging fashion items and finding new
owners for our old garments!

Please bring

Date _____   ☐ Yourself, some clothes and a happy mood
Time _____   ☐ Something to drink
Place _____ ☐ Something to snack

SWAP PARTY INVITE

Dear _____

You and the clothes that you don't need anymore are invited to _____'s
swap party, where we will have fun by exchanging fashion items and finding
new owners for our old garments!

Please bring

Date _____   ☐ Yourself, some clothes and a happy mood

Time _____   ☐ Something to drink

Place _____ ☐ Something to snack

SWAP PARTY INVITE

Dear _____

You and the clothes that you don't need anymore are invited to _____'s
swap party, where we will have fun by exchanging fashion items and finding
new owners for our old garments!

Please bring

Date _____   ☐ Yourself, some clothes and a happy mood

Time _____   ☐ Something to drink

Place _____ ☐ Something to snack

SUBSTITUTES FOR SHOPPING

Quench your craving to shop by listing all
the other fun things you can do instead!

TO DO:
* bake cookies
* CLEAN YOUR CLOSET

Still feeling a huge urge to shop?
Get yourself some shopping bags here!

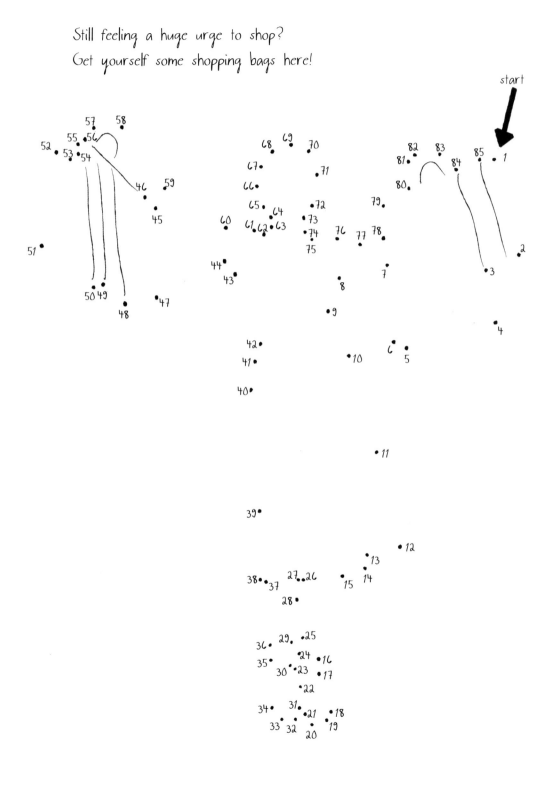

start

T-SHIRT TRANSFORMATIONS

TAKE your old t-shirts out of the closet and give them a new, restyled life with these DIY instructions!

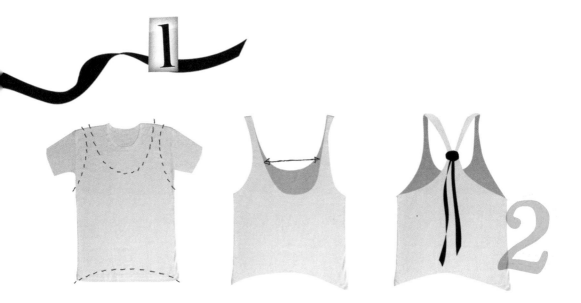

Here's how to make an easy crop top: Lay a big tee on the floor. Cut the sleeves out and use your scissors to alter the neck and hemline as well. For additional oomph, cut out the neck opening at the back lower than the front. Turn the shirt over and tie the back together with a ribbon of your choice. Leave its ends hanging at the back for an elegant appeal, and voila, you've got yourself a new top!

cut open the
seam of the sleeve

Decorate a shirt with a two-layer fringe! For this, you need two old t-shirts with the same kind of neckline, either with a V or an O shape. Cut out the collar and cut off one sleeve from the other shirt. After you have cut them off from the tee, make cuts up their hems to make your fringe.

Stretch out the fringes to make them curl. Take the other shirt and place the cut-off sleeve right below its neckline and attach with pins. Then lay the collar part on top of it, pin and sew both of the layers on the shirt. If you want only one layer of fringe, use only the fringed neckline and sew it onto the other shirt.

DIY design by Anne Hollabaugh
Wobisobi.blogspot.com

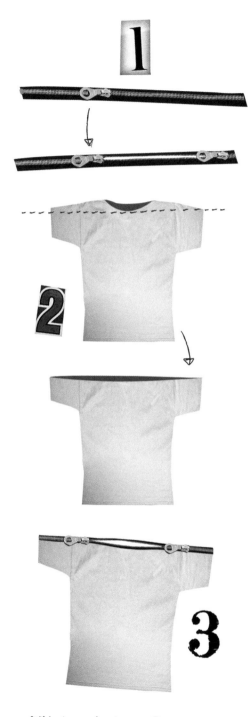

Here's how to make a trendy zipper shirt: Take a large T-shirt and a 55-60 cm long zipper. You will also need one extra zipper slider. Cut off the little stopper at the end of the zipper and pull the extra zipper through. Take the shirt and make a straight cut through the top, cutting through the sleeves, shoulder seams and cutting off the neckband as well. After this, your shirt should have the shape of a T.

Turn the shirt inside out and place the zipper upside down, straight across the top of the shirt, so that the front side of the zipper is facing the front of the fabric. Attach the zipper to the shirt with pins and cut the sleeves to fit the length of the zipper. Sew the sides of the zipper onto the shirt to create new shoulder seams with it. Finish by making a hole for your neck, simply by opening the zipper from the middle.

Note: You can neaten the edges of the sleeve openings by folding 1 cm of the fabric from each side inwards and sewing before attaching the zipper.

DIY design by Laura Pifer
Trashtocouture.com

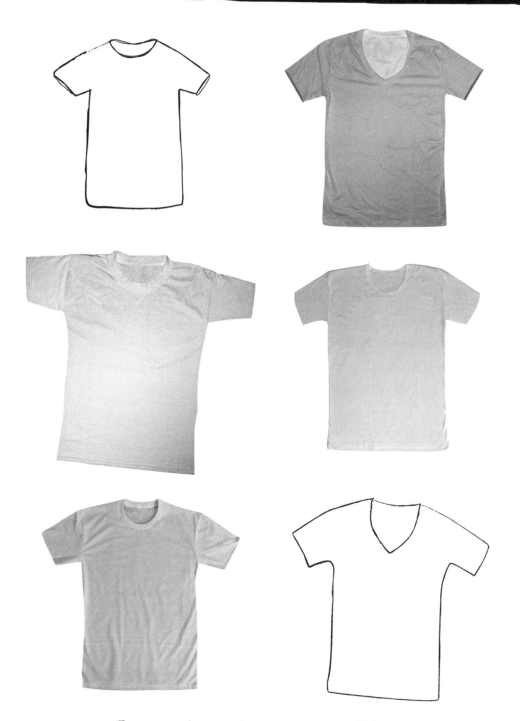

There are dozens of ways to revamp T-shirts.
Alternate these shirts with some ideas of your own!

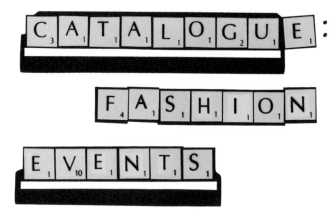

CATALOGUE:

FASHION

EVENTS

WACKY outfits, extraordinary designs and original ideas for styling; that's what fashion events are made of. Complete this list of happenings that will stir your imagination!

MY LOCAL EVENTS

FASHION WEEKS

Look up the dates of these fashion events and add them to your calendar!

New York: _____

London: _____

_____

_____

_____

_____

_____

_____

Milan: _____

Paris: _____

_____

_____

_____

_____

_____

_____

OTHER IMPORTANT DATES

- Vogue September issue for winter
& fall fashion: in stores in August
- Vogue March issue for spring
fashion in stores in February
Note: Also other magazines tend
to bring their most important issues
out at these times!

_____

_____

_____

_____

_____

_____

_____

MY PERSONAL FASHION WEEK

KEEP TRACK of your outfits
for one week to see what you actually wear.
Draw, photograph or describe your outfits here!

Comments: _____

_____

_____

_____

_____

DATE ⌐⌐⌐⌐⌐⌐

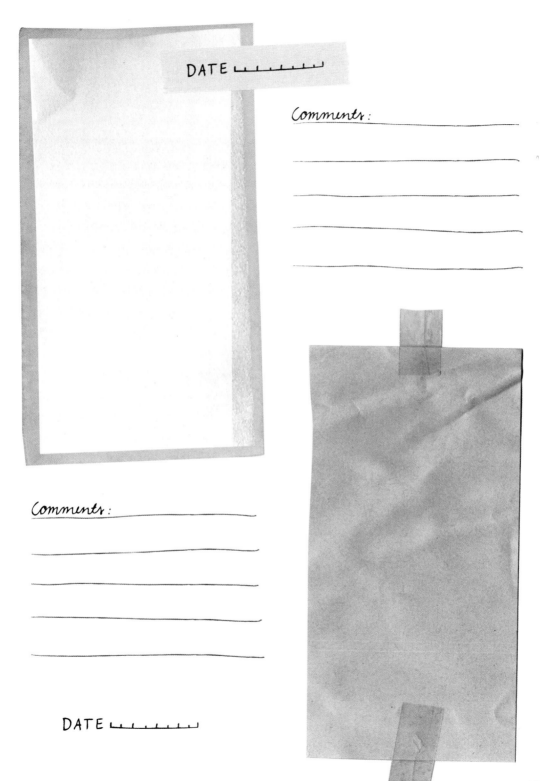

DATE ⌐└┴┴┴┴┴┴┘

Comments :

Comments :

DATE ⌐└┴┴┴┴┴┘

Comments:

Comments:

DATE ⌞⌞⌞⌞⌞⌞⌞⌞

Comments :

_____

_____

_____

_____

_____

Comments :

_____

_____

_____

_____

_____

AFTERMATH
CONCLUSIONS

This week my style was...

☐ Simple	☐ down-to-earth	☐ sportive
☐ CLASSIC	☐ COLORFUL	☐ feminine
☐ EXPERIMENTAL	☐ PRACTICAL	☐ original
☐ IMAGINATIVE	☐ very 'me'	☐ ROCK'N'ROLL!

My favorite look was _____

because _____

_____

I noticed that _____

_____

In the future I will _____

_____

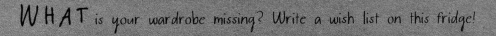

WHAT is your wardrobe missing? Write a wish list on this fridge!

CATALOGUE:
MY FAVORITE
BLOGS

WHEN in need of styling tips, check what your fellow fashionistas are doing online; make a list of blogs that are closest to your own style and search them for new ideas!

BLOG 1 : www.

Description:

The nicest thing about this blog:

BLOG 2: www.

Description:

The best time to read this blog:

BLOG 3: www. [   ]

Description:

This blog inspires to...

BLOG 4: www. [   ]

Description:

This blog is fab because...

BLOG 5: www. [   ]

Description:

This blog gives ideas for...

BLOG 6: www. [   ]

Description:

The best thing about this blog:

Style Spy

Become a **STYLE SPY**: Go on a hunt for exciting outfits and sketch or photograph your most thrilling finds to create a collection of inspiration for your own style!

WHAT YOU NEED
- camera
- pencil
- paper for notes

TIPS for good spying spots:
- parks on sunny days
- street cafés
- festivals
- big squares in city centers
- windows of shopping malls
- vintage markets

Found at:

This outfit caught my attention with its _____

_____

It inspires me because _____

_____

The best elements in it are _____

_____

I could apply them to my own style by _____

_____

This outfit caught my attention with its _____

_____

It inspires me because _____

_____

The best elements in it are _____

_____

I could apply them to my own style by _____

_____

Found at:

Found at:

This outfit caught my attention with its _____

_____

It inspires me because _____

_____

The best elements in it are _____

_____

I could apply them to my own style by _____

_____

This outfit caught my attention with its _____

_____

It inspires me because _____

_____

The best elements in it are _____

_____

I could apply them to my own style by _____

_____

This outfit caught my attention with its _____

_____

It inspires me because _____

_____

The best elements in it are _____

_____

I could apply them to my own style by _____

_____

Found at:

GUEST FEATURE

ASK a *friend* to describe your
fashion self and fill in these gaps:

Completed by: _____

We have known each other for

When thinking of you, these **THREE WORDS** are the ones that *pop* into my

mind:

When we met, your style was

These days, your *style* is

and I often see you wearing

If your style was a **SONG**, it would be

If it was a perfume, it would smell like

I couldn't imagine you wearing

because

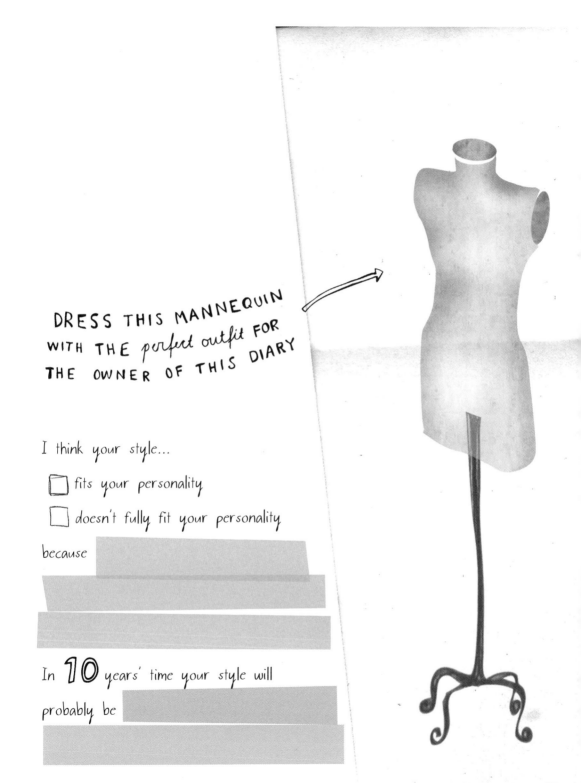

DRESS THIS MANNEQUIN
WITH THE *perfect outfit* FOR
THE OWNER OF THIS DIARY

I think your style...

☐ fits your personality

☐ doesn't fully fit your personality

because

In **10** years' time your style will
probably be

"Fashion is
about
dressing according
to what's
fashionable.
Style is
more about
being yourself."

- Oscar de la Renta

WHAT DOES STYLE MEAN TO YOU?

Write down your answer:

STYLE (PUZZLE)

LET'S play a little game: the first 3 words you find in this puzzle describe your style. Which words do you get?

```
P R A C T I C A L N U I N E E S
S U E I F N O I A N T T U V L H
D U N C M L A U S A C D I A T G
L E O K L S B G E S O T T O I E
U G T N N E P N A W A N G R M N
F A T C Y I C O N V E L L R E A
H T B R I G H T R M A Y C G L B
T N I L P T O E I T A R D T E R
U I E F U E S R H C I E T C S U
O V A K A N E I D S G V R X S P
Y R A R O P M E T N O C E U E O
F L T C X P E P I R A P N N L I
M H P E F A S T K R A D D I P E
O M O D E S T T F O S S Y Q M B
C C O L O U R F U L U T N U I A
S O Q U C F M O N O T O N E S I
```

There are 34 words hidden in this puzzle. Can you find them all?
Find the solutions on page 156.

1 WORD:

On a scale of one to ten, how well does this word actually describe your style? Circle your choice.

1 2 3 4 5 6 7 8 9 10

2 WORD:

1 2 3 4 5 6 7 8 9 10

3 WORD:

1 2 3 4 5 6 7 8 9 10

DATE WITH A DESIGNER

Plan a date with a designer extraordinaire
you have always wanted to meet!

Paste a picture of one of
your favorite designs from
him/her here!

If I could have a meeting with a fashion designer, I would like to meet

_____

because _____

_____

_____

_____

We would go ☐ for tea/coffee

☐ for lunch

☐ to an art exhibition

☐ other: what? _____

and talk about _____

_____

_____

_____

_____

_____

I would also like to ask him/her _____

_____

_____

_____

_____

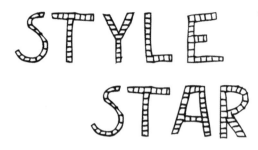

STYLE STAR

Some stars shine brighter than others
thanks to their dazzling style. Whose
sense of fashion do you admire? Marilyn Monroe's,
Lady Gaga's, James Dean's or somebody else's?
Choose your favorite fashion icon and write a
tribute to him/her.

Fill this page with inspiring images
showing your fashion icon's style.

Dear

This is an **APPLAUSE** to your style, which stands out

because

and

Your sense of *fashion* inspires me to

and I L♥VE the way you wear

Thanks to you I, too, have gratefully adopted

into my wardrobe.

Thank you for all the *inspiration*!

Yours truly,

103

TIME TRAVEL

DO YOU fancy the radiant colors of the 70s, the bohemian vibes of the 60s or the cloche hats from the 20s? Travel back in time to your favorite style period and document your trip here!

Write your desired year here!

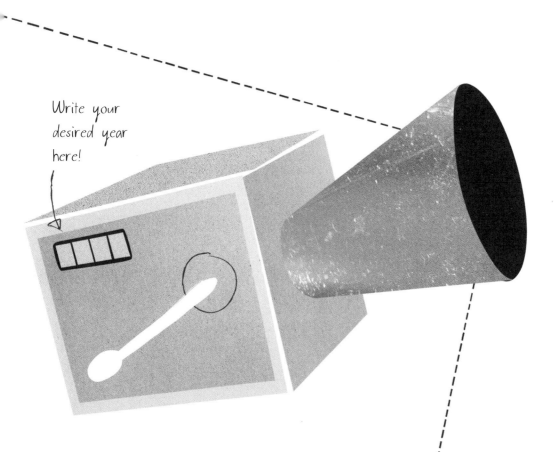

Looks like you got yourself a souvenir, too! Which fashion item did you bring from your trip? Draw a miniature of it inside this bag!

Complete this page with inspiring style images from your trip.

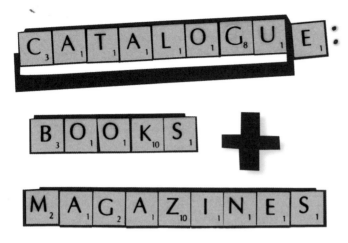

CATALOGUE:

BOOKS + MAGAZINES

WHEN your outfit feels like a bore, all you might need is a bit of reinventing. Draw the covers of the books and fashion magazines that give you the best outfit ideas.

Name: _____

Great inspiration for _____

_____

I would recommended it to _____

_____

Name: _____

I like reading this when _____

_____

It has good tips for _____

_____

Name: _____

A good read when in need of _____

_____

I would recommend it to _____

_____

Name: _____

The thing I most like about this is _____

_____

It has good tips for _____

_____

Name: _____

Great inspiration for _____

_____

I would recommend it to _____

_____

Name: _____

I like reading this when _____

_____

It inspires me to _____

_____

TRENDSPOTTING

SCOUT for TRENDS with a pair of scissors & a pile of magazines and create an inspiration collage to spice up your *looks* with trends that suit your personality!

MY FAVORITE SHOPS

Draw images of the top three of your favorite shops on this street!

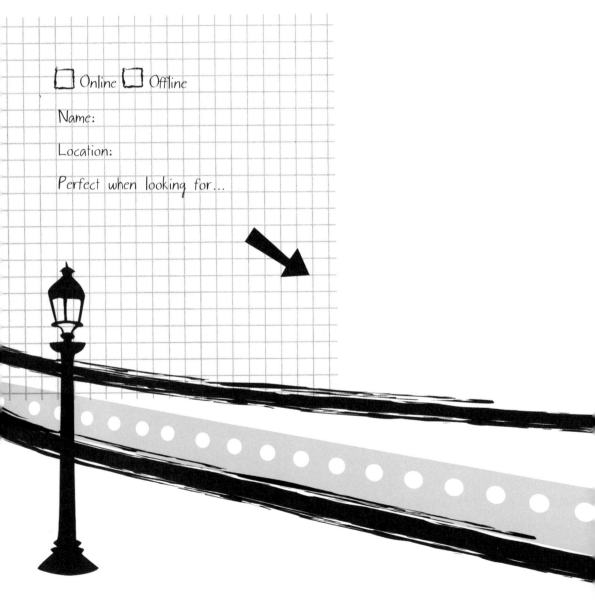

☐ Online ☐ Offline

Name:

Location:

Perfect when looking for...

☐ Online ☐ Offline

Name:

Location:

Perfect when looking for...

☐ Online ☐ Offline

Name:

Location:

Perfect when looking for...

WHEN IN ROME

TASTES vary from country to country.
Broaden your perspective and get inspired by
asking three foreigners what is considered to
be stylish in their countries!

Dear _____

Greetings from _____ ,

where people love wearing

_____

_____

_____

We think it's stylish to

_____

_____

_____

From:

POSTAGE REVENUE 4ᴰ
E R

Greetings from _____,
the land where wearing

_____

_____

is extremely hip. You might also

want to try _____

_____

From:

Hello from _____,
the land where the fashion crowds

dress in _____

_____

and think that it is an absolute must

to _____

_____

From:

SIGNATURE ITEMS

Which items in your wardrobe are the most typically you?
Put a spotlight on five of your most worn signature items
by drawing them here!

Tip: Not sure what your signature pieces are?
Ask your friends which items they
recognise you by!

This _____ is very me because _____

_____

_____

This _____ looks like me because _____

_____

_____

This _____ looks typically me thanks to its _____

_____

_____

This _____ is very me because _____

_____

_____

This _____ is typically me because _____

_____

_____

AFTERMATH:
CONCLUSIONS

Your signature items can give an inkling of
what your personal style is made of. Can you
spot similarities between them? Note down the
characteristics they share:

Colors: _____

Silhouettes: _____

Design details: _____

Other characteristics: _____

_____

My signature items are ☐ all completely different
☐ somewhat similar
☐ very similar

They ☐ give a good idea of what my style is like.
☐ don't really give the right impression of
my style, because _____

_____

_____

WHICH STYLE ELEMENTS ARE TIMELESS TO YOU?

Write down your answer:

*"Fashions fade,
but style
is eternal"*

— YVESSAINTLAURENT

if I could have anything...

Confess your biggest fashion cravings!

If I could get any fashion item in the world, I would like to have

_____

_____

because _____

_____

_____

_____

_____

_____

_____

_____

Draw or paste images
of your ultimate dream
item(s) here!

PRINT DESIGN

CREATE your own print design; take a
pen and fill this spread with geometrical shapes,
flowers or any other patterns you like!

START HERE

FASHION

Solve these stylish sudoku puzzles using the listed items so that each row, column and 3x3 box will contain the 9 different fashion items exactly once.

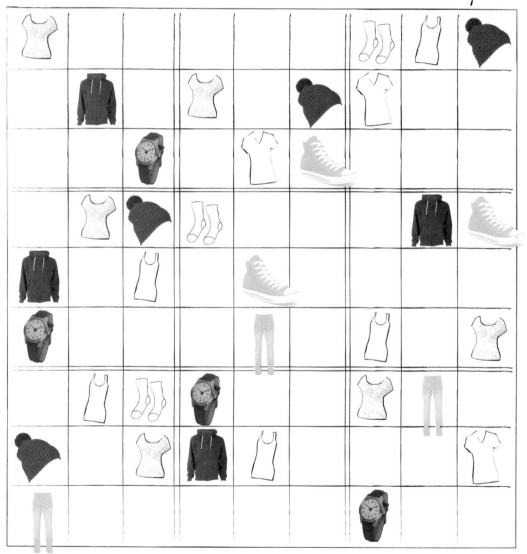

SUDOKU

Practice with basic garments on the left and top your skills with high fashion items on the right! Find the solutions on page 157.

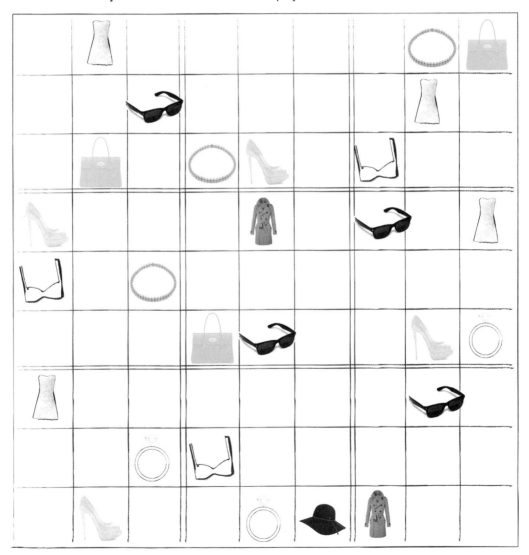

MULTIFUNCTIONAL FASHION

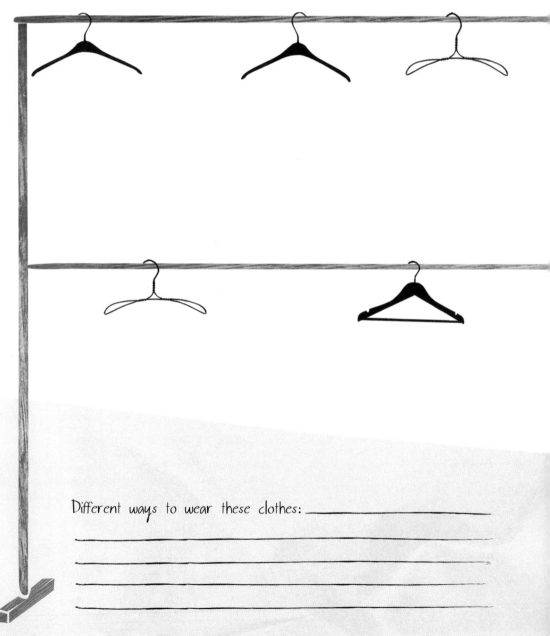

Different ways to wear these clothes: _____

_____

_____

_____

_____

The smartest garments can be worn in different ways and on many occasions. Hang the most multifunctional items in your wardrobe on this rack and write down as many different ways of wearing them as you can think of!

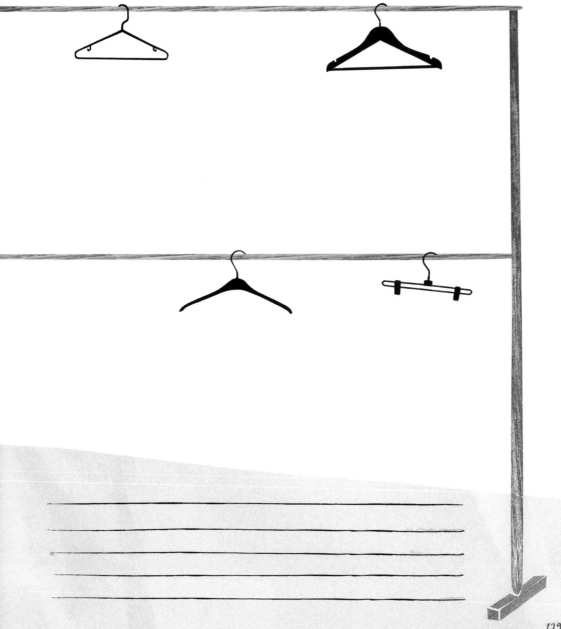

MY CAPSULE COLLECTION

A capsule collection is a small selection of garments that can be easily combined into many different outfits. A typical capsule collection consists of *classics* such as a trench coat, white T-shirt and a little black dress, but what does your own capsule collection look like?

Dive into your wardrobe and pull out your most worn items, the cornerstones of your style. Create your **PERSONAL** capsule collection by drawing those items on this doll and see what kind of different outfits you can create with them!

ITEM:

GOES WELL WITH:

ITEM:

GOES WELL WITH:

ITEM:

GOES WELL WITH:

ITEM:

GOES WELL WITH:

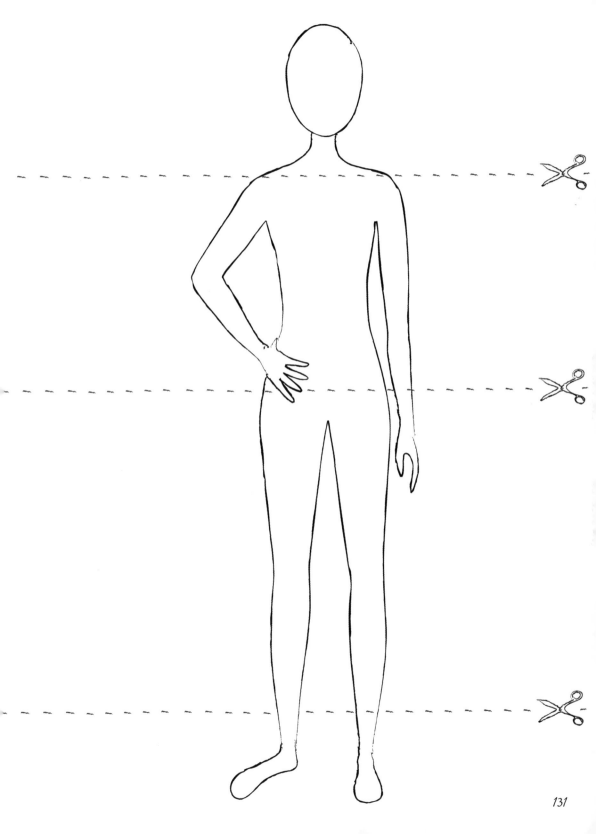

ITEM:

GOES WELL WITH:

ITEM:

GOES WELL WITH:

ITEM:

GOES WELL WITH:

ITEM:

GOES WELL WITH:

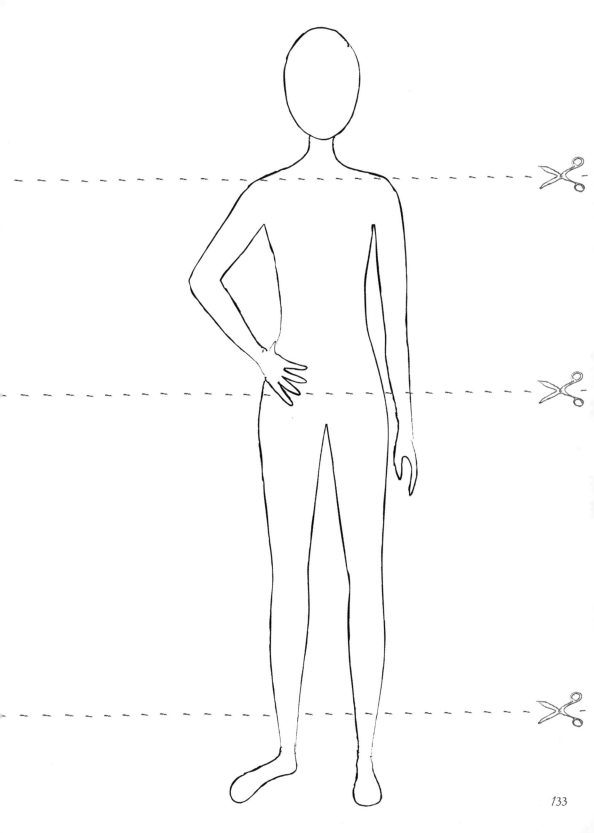

ITEM:

GOES WELL WITH:

ITEM:

GOES WELL WITH:

ITEM:

GOES WELL WITH:

ITEM:

GOES WELL WITH:

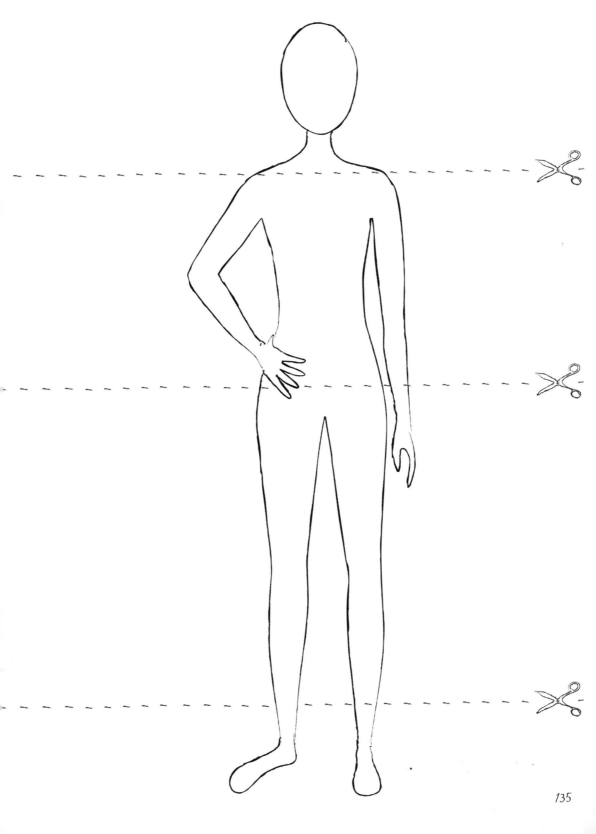

ITEM:

GOES WELL WITH:

ITEM:

GOES WELL WITH:

ITEM:

GOES WELL WITH:

ITEM:

GOES WELL WITH:

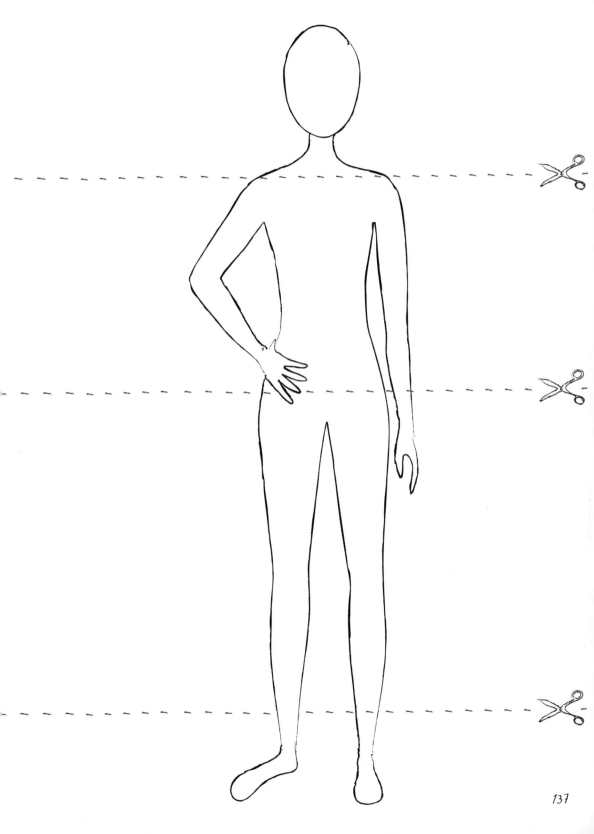

137

"I really like
to be able
     to have variety
and to try
different things
     - that's the beauty
of fashion."

- Leighton Meester

WHAT IS THE BEAUTY OF FASHION TO YOU?

Write down your answer:

STATEMENT SHIRT

MAKE A STATEMENT:

stamp your slogan on this shirt!

SMART TIPS
+ TRICKS

COLLECT functional fashion tips to ease your dress-up dilemmas. Source blogs, consult fashion magazines or ask the most practical people you know to share their tricks with you!

When you want to shop smartly...

When you don't know what to wear...

When you want to stay cool...

...and keep warm!

Other words of wisdom:

Glue an envelope here and fill it with
DIY instructions and ideas for
re-using your old clothes!

WHAT IS IN YOUR SUITCASE?

PACKING is always a challenge, as you can bring only a limited amount of garments to be worn in many different ways. Make a packing list and fill this suitcase with the most essential items that should travel everywhere with you!

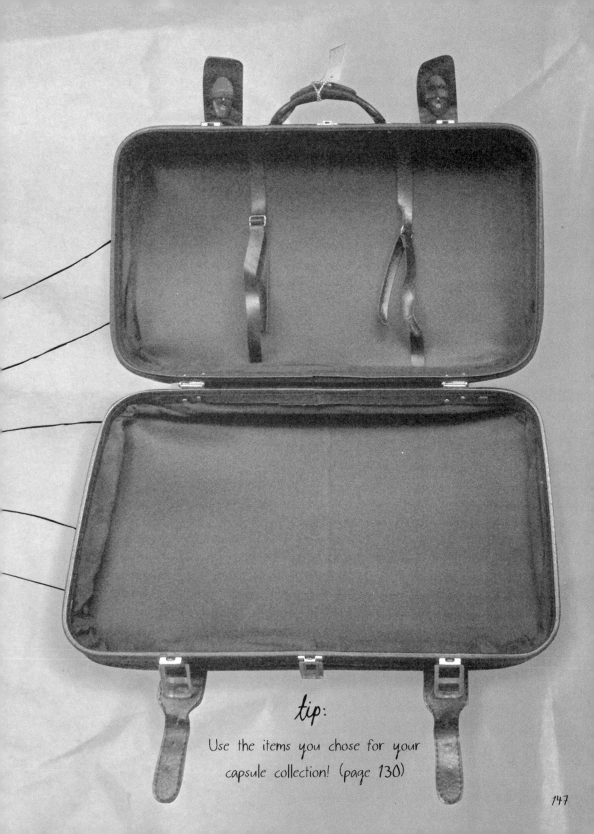

tip:

Use the items you chose for your
capsule collection! (page 130)

RECIPE TO MY STYLE

LEARN to cook up outfits that are uniquely you by completing this quick recipe to your personal style and using it as a style guide when shopping!

COLOURS

Add your top 5 favorite colors to wear...

...and add a few neutral tones to combine them with:

SILHOUETTES

Circle the shape that is closest to your silhouette!

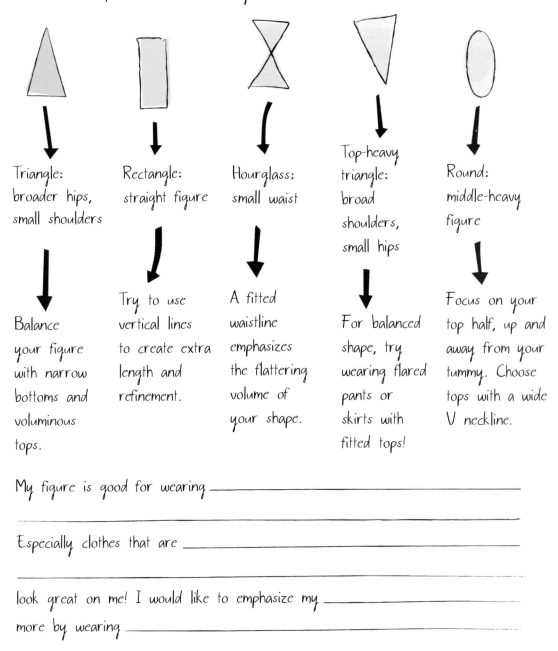

Triangle: broader hips, small shoulders

Rectangle: straight figure

Hourglass: small waist

Top-heavy triangle: broad shoulders, small hips

Round: middle-heavy figure

Balance your figure with narrow bottoms and voluminous tops.

Try to use vertical lines to create extra length and refinement.

A fitted waistline emphasizes the flattering volume of your shape.

For balanced shape, try wearing flared pants or skirts with fitted tops!

Focus on your top half, up and away from your tummy. Choose tops with a wide V neckline.

My figure is good for wearing _____

_____

Especially clothes that are _____

_____

look great on me! I would like to emphasize my _____
more by wearing _____

COMPLEMENTING CUTS

Do you like scoops, V-necks or polos the best?
Draw three necklines that flatter you most.

Flared jeans, straight pants, leggings and mini skirts - what
kind of bottoms fit your body and personality? Dress these
legs with three of your favorite types of bottoms!

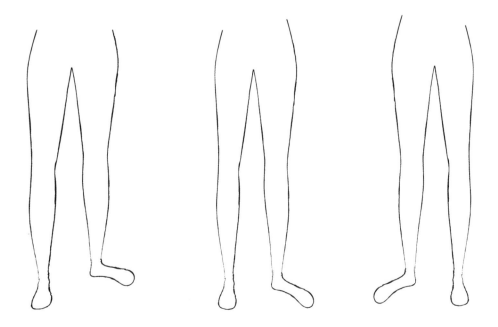

MATERIALS

Choose your materials based on what's important for you:

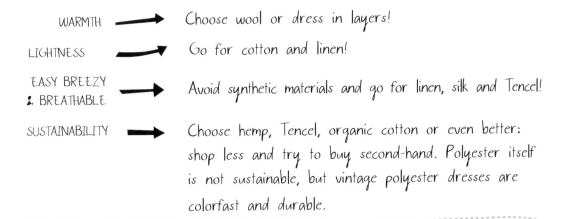

WARMTH ⟶ Choose wool or dress in layers!

LIGHTNESS ⟶ Go for cotton and linen!

EASY BREEZY & BREATHABLE ⟶ Avoid synthetic materials and go for linen, silk and Tencel!

SUSTAINABILITY ⟶ Choose hemp, Tencel, organic cotton or even better: shop less and try to buy second-hand. Polyester itself is not sustainable, but vintage polyester dresses are colorfast and durable.

DESIGN DETAILS

Bows and lace or sequin glacé - which design details and ornaments tickle your style taste buds? Doodle examples of them here!

SHOPPING LIST

List the clothes that are missing from your wardrobe.
Follow the dashed line to cut these pages out to be
folded inside your pocket for your next shopping spree!

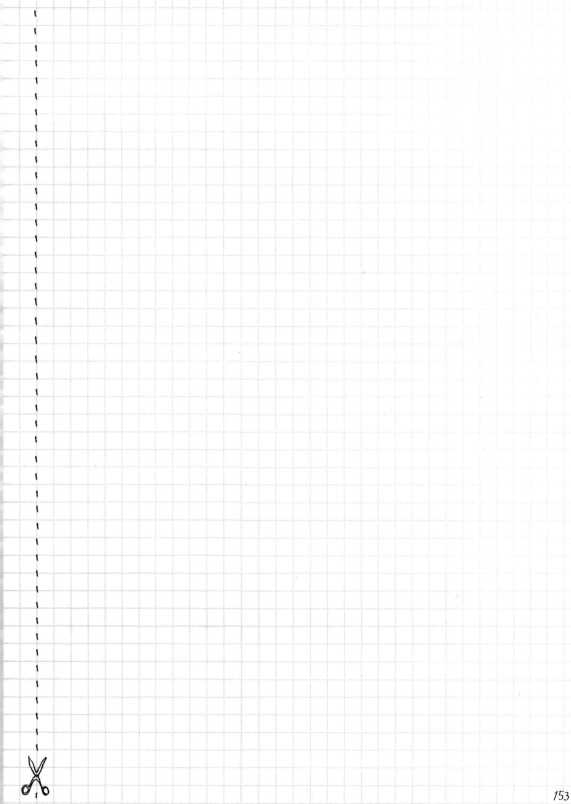

COMPLIMENT COLLECTOR

We all love flattering words! Write down the best compliments you have ever gotten to cheer you up on a bad-outfit day.

TAKE A COMPLIMENT

(They're free!)

Spread some sweet words and cut these out to be given to friends and strangers!

I have a style crush on you!

You are my style hero!

You set the trend!

That dress really suits you!

You look fantastic!

You have the cutest smile :-)

Love what you're wearing!

You look gorgeous!

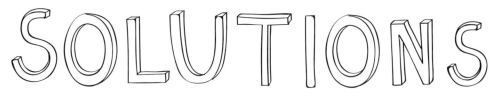

SOLUTIONS

STYLE (PUZZLE)

```
P R A C T I C A L N U I N E E S
S U E I F N O I A N T T U V L H
D U N C M L A U S A C D I A T G
L E O K L S B G E S O T T O I E
U G T N N E P N A W A N G R M N
F A T C Y I C O N V E L L R E A
H T B R I G H T R M A Y C G L B
T N I L P T O E I T A R D T E R
U I E F U E S R H C I E T C S U
O V A K A N E I D S G V R X S P
Y R A R O P M E T N O C E U E O
F L T C X P E P I R A P N N L I
M H P E F A S T K R A D D I P E
O M O D E S T T F O S S Y Q M B
C C O L O U R F U L U T N U I A
S O Q U C F M O N O T O N E S I
```

Practical	Girly	Modest	Youthful	Experimental
Punk	Urban	Soft	Outspoken	Contemporary
Eclectic	Simple	Dark	Classic	Down-to-earth
Casual	Unique	Bright	Posh	Cutting edge
Neat	Trendy	Artistic	Safe	Conservative
Goth	Monotone	Vintage	Extravagant	Sportive
Timeless	Colourful	Comfy	Androgynous	

FASHION SUDOKU

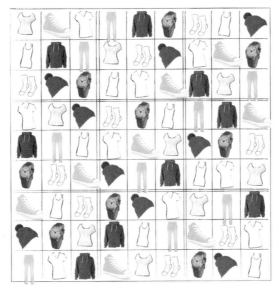

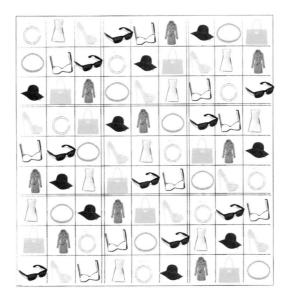

CONTENTS

DOCUMENT YOUR FASHION LIFE

SURVIVALOGUE

ALTERNATIVE FASHION ACTIVITIES

DISCOVER YOUR TASTE

BECOME YOUR OWN STYLE GURU

ABOUT
LAURA DE JONG
AND EMMI OJALA

This diary is a labour of love and collaboration between Laura de Jong and Emmi Ojala. The girls found each other on their quest for a more creative, sustainable and quality-driven fashion industry, when Laura founded the *free fashion challenge* as her graduation project for the Amsterdam Fashion Institute. In this challenge, people stop shopping for 365 days to experience fashion beyond consumption. Emmi, a fashion graduate herself, joined the first sequence of the *free fashion challenge* and after that year of not shopping, the girls decided to collaborate in hopes of inspiring others to discover the creativity of fashion outside the cycle of consumption. Currently, Laura works as a freelance communication and content specialist in the field of fashion, lifestyle and sustainability. After launching a fashion magazine called *dear fashion journal*, Emmi now works as a freelance editor and illustrator in the field of fashion, art and lifestyle.

A note from the authors/illustrators:

A big thank you to all those who reviewed our work, joined us in brainstorms, cooked us couscous and gave their support on late working nights!

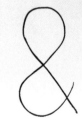

Emmi Ojala
www.emmiojala.eu

Laura de Jong
www.lauradejong.com

PS. Come say hello to us at Facebook.com/DearFashionDiary or Twitter.com/DearFashionBook